Moses
Youth Study Book

Moses:
In the Footsteps of the Reluctant Prophet

Moses
978-1-5018-0788-6 *Hardcover with jacket*
978-1-5018-0789-3 *e-Book*
978-1-5018-0790-9 *Large Print*

Moses: DVD
978-1-5018-0793-0

Moses: Leader Guide
978-1-5018-0791-6
978-1-5018-0792-3 *e-Book*

Moses: Youth Study Book
978-1-5018-0800-5
978-1-5018-0801-2 *e-Book*

Moses: Children's Leader Guide
978-1-5018-0802-9

Also by Adam Hamilton

24 Hours That Changed the World

Christianity and World Religions

Christianity's Family Tree

Confronting the Controversies

Creed

Enough

Final Words from the Cross

Forgiveness

Half Truths

John

Leading Beyond the Walls

Love to Stay

Making Sense of the Bible

Not a Silent Night

Revival

Seeing Gray in a World of Black and White

Selling Swimsuits in the Arctic

Speaking Well

The Call

The Journey

The Way

Unleashing the Word

When Christians Get It Wrong

Why?

For more information, visit www.AdamHamilton.org.

ADAM HAMILTON

MOSES

In the Footsteps of the
RELUCTANT PROPHET

Youth Study Book
by Josh Tinley

Abingdon Press / Nashville

Moses:
In the Footsteps of the Reluctant Prophet
Youth Study Book

Copyright © 2017 Abingdon Press
All rights reserved.

This book is printed on elemental chlorine-free paper.

978-1-5018-0800-5

Scripture quotations are from the Common English Bible. Copyright © 2011 by the Common English Bible. All rights reserved. Used by permission. www.CommonEnglishBible.com.

17 18 19 20 21 22 23 24 25 26 — 10 9 8 7 6 5 4 3 2 1
MANUFACTURED IN THE UNITED STATES OF AMERICA

CONTENTS

Introduction. 7

1. The Birth of Moses. 9

2. Two Moments That Defined the Man. 17

3. The Exodus. 25

4. The Ten Commandments. 37

5. Lessons from the Wilderness. 47

6. Don't Forget . . . Pass It On 57

INTRODUCTION

Moses

The Bible is likely the most-read book in history, and it is full of figures that are household names—Abraham, Sarah, Jacob, David, Mary, Peter, Paul, and, well, Jesus. But no list of famous Bible people is complete without Moses.

Moses is the central figure in four of the Bible's first five books; in fact, the first five books of the Bible, often are called the "Books of Moses." Moses' name became synonymous with the Jewish law; even Jesus says "Moses" to refer to the Old Testament law. And Moses, along with Elijah, was one of the two people to join Jesus during his Transfiguration (see Mark 9:2-8).

Moses has been the subject of many classic works of art and Hollywood films. And he has been an inspiration and symbol for people around the world who have strived for freedom from slavery and oppression. We can learn a great deal from this man who had such an impact on Scripture, history, faith, and culture.

This six-session study for youth will examine Moses' entire story, from his birth through his remarkable life to his death. The study is based upon *Moses: In the Footsteps of the Reluctant Prophet* by Adam Hamilton.

Using This Book

Each session in this Youth Study Book begins with some thoughts and information about Moses, to get you reading and thinking. Next, there will be a variety of activities and discussion starters. Next to each activity is an estimate of how long it will take and a list of necessary supplies, when applicable. The activities add up to about fifty minutes, but they can be tailored to fit the needs of your group. Every session includes an opening activity and prayer, and a closing activity and prayer

The hope is that, as you work through these six sessions, you will be inspired by the story of Moses and, like the Israelites he led, set out to create your own story.

1.

THE BIRTH OF MOSES

An Origin Story Fit for a Superhero

Moses was born to an Israelite woman named Jochebed during a tumultuous time for the Israelites in Egypt. The Israelites were descendants of Jacob, who was also known by the name of Israel. Jacob moved his entire family from Canaan to Egypt after his son Joseph acquired a position of power under the Egyptian pharaoh and saved the entire region from a seven-year famine. Things went well for Jacob's family in Egypt for decades. But eventually, as Jacob's descendants become more numerous and the remembrance of Joseph's deeds was lost to history, the Egyptian pharaoh came to see the Israelites, or Hebrews, as a threat.

Pharaoh forced the Israelites into hard labor and put them to work building new cities. As their population continued growing, he ordered two Hebrew midwives to kill all Israelite baby boys as they were being born. When the midwives deceived Pharaoh to avoid killing any babies, Pharaoh ordered all Israelite baby boys to be thrown into the Nile River.

Moses was born during this time. His mother hid him as long as she could to protect him. When she could hide him no longer, she placed him in a basket and set him in among the reeds near the riverbank. There he was discovered by Pharaoh's daughter, who raised Moses as her own. Though he was Hebrew, Moses grew up as Egyptian royalty. Moses' older sister offered to find for Pharaoh's daughter a Hebrew woman who could nurse the baby. The nursing job, of course, went to Moses' mother, allowing her to be a part of her child's life.

Exodus 2:1-10, which tells us about Moses' birth, doesn't mention God. But God's hand is nonetheless at work in the story. We see God in the courage of Moses' mother, who took desperate measures to protect her son. We see God in Pharaoh's daughter, the foreign princess who rescued Moses and raised him as her own. And we see God in Moses' sister, who found a way to keep the family together. Even amid the discord and uncertainty, God is present and active.

A Land of Pyramids

The first thing that comes to mind when many people think of ancient Egypt is pyramids. Some even assume that the Israelite slaves were responsible for building these pyramids. In reality, the Egyptians built their pyramids long before the time of Moses. But pyramids and other great monuments were part of the Egyptian environment in which Moses and the other Israelites lived.

In Egyptian belief, the pyramids served as vehicles that would take the Egyptian pharaohs—along with their families, servants, and possessions—into the afterlife. Some historians have suggested that Egyptians believed the pyramids even propelled the pharaohs to the realm of the gods. These magnificent structures signified that the Egyptians looked upon their leaders with reverence, the type of reverence that the Israelites reserved for their God.

Moses was born into a nation of slaves but grew up in the household of a ruler who was revered like a god. He belonged to two peoples that were at odds with each other. But God had big plans for him.

Session 1 Activities

Opening Activity: Word Association (10 minutes)

Supplies: a markerboard or large sheet of paper, markers

Divide a markerboard or large sheet of paper into three columns. Title the first "Ancient Egypt"; title the second "Moses"; and title the third "The Exodus."

Have participants name the first thing that comes to mind when they hear "Ancient Egypt." Record these in the first column. (It is fine if some answers are repeated.) Do the same with "Moses" and "The Exodus."

With these terms in mind, divide into teams of three or four. Have each team answer each of the following questions:

1. What is something that you know for sure about Moses and the story of the Israelites' escape from Egypt?
2. What is one question that you have about Moses and the story of the Israelites' escape from Egypt?

Over the next six sessions you will learn about several different aspects of Moses' life and of the ancient Israelites' saga. More importantly, you'll discover how God was at work in these ancient stories and how the lessons they teach us apply to our lives and faith today.

Opening Prayer

Lord, guide us during our time together today and throughout this study. Open our minds and hearts so that we might understand what you have to say to us through the story of Moses and the ancient Israelites. Thank you for the wisdom and example of our ancestors in faith and for this time we have to learn about them. Amen.

Pyramid Contest (10 minutes)

Supplies: assorted sets of materials for building pyramids

Divide participants into groups of three or four. Challenge each group to build a pyramid, with each group using a different set of materials. One group

11

could have paper cups, another could have drinking straws, and another children's building blocks. Give each group two minutes to construct a pyramid from the materials provided. After two minutes, judge the pyramids and declare two winners: one for the highest pyramid and one for the strongest and sturdiest.

The first thing that comes to mind when many people think of Egypt is pyramids. The Great Pyramids are the best known landmarks in Egypt and are among the best known in all the world. Discuss:

- What do you know, or think you know, about the Egyptian pyramids?
- Which of these things are you certain of? Which are you not sure about?

Many people mistakenly are under the impression that Hebrew slaves built the Great Pyramids in Egypt. This idea has been reinforced by movie portrayals of Moses' story, such as *The Prince of Egypt* and *Exodus: Gods and Kings*. But there is no historical evidence that Hebrew slaves, or slaves of any kind, built the pyramids. The pyramids most likely were built by a workforce of farmers during the flood season when farming wasn't possible. By the time of Moses, the pyramids probably had been standing for a thousand years.

Even though the ancient Israelites weren't responsible for building the pyramids, the presence of the pyramids tells us about the Egyptian culture in which God's people lived. The pyramids were believed to function as "resurrection machines," guiding pharaohs and others buried in them into the afterlife and even to godly status. Discuss:

- People today who visit the pyramids in Egypt stand in awe of their size, their durability, and the precision with which they were built. How do you think the ancient Israelites reacted when they first encountered the Egyptian pyramids?
- What do the pyramids tell us about how the Egyptians viewed their leaders?
- How was this view of the Egyptian pharaoh at odds with the faith of God's people?

The Backstory (5 minutes)

Supplies: Bibles are optional

Moses was born into a world where the Israelites were slaves in Egypt, and his crowning achievement was freeing his people from slavery. But how did they end up enslaved in the first place? We can find the answer to this question in the Book of Genesis and the story of Joseph. Ask:

- What do you know about Joseph (the Joseph in the Old Testament, not Jesus' adoptive father)?
- What would you like to know about him?

Read aloud the following paragraphs:

> Joseph is perhaps best known for the colorful coat that his father, Jacob, gave him. Joseph was his father's favorite son, and his ten older brothers were jealous and resentful. At first plotting to kill Joseph, his brothers instead sold him into slavery. Joseph ended up in Egypt. Thanks to his ability to interpret dreams, Joseph worked his way out of slavery and eventually—after being wrongly convicted and imprisoned—became one of Pharaoh's top advisors.

> Joseph secured his advisory role when he interpreted a dream of Pharaoh's that involved seven fat and seven slender cattle. The dream told Joseph that there would be seven years of plenty followed by seven years of famine. By interpreting this dream, Joseph was able to guide Egypt through the seven-year famine and was even able to provide food for other nations in the region. From Canaan, Joseph's brothers traveled to Egypt seeking food. In Egypt, they appeared before Joseph, not knowing he was their brother. After some back-and-forth and trickery, which you can read about in Genesis 42–45, Joseph moved his entire family to Egypt—his father Jacob, his brothers, and their families. Joseph's family prospered in Egypt until their descendants became so numerous that a new pharaoh regarded them as a threat.

Discuss:

- What do you know about how your family came to live in this community or this country? What circumstances led them here?

- How might God have been at work in the story of Joseph and his family?
- How has God been at work in the story of your family, bringing them to where they are today?

Moses: The Origin Story (10 minutes)

Supplies: Bibles, a markerboard or large sheet of paper, markers

Most great heroes have an interesting origin story. Moses is no different. Read aloud Exodus 1:8-14, 22. Discuss:

- Why did Pharaoh feel threatened by the Israelites?
- What did he do in response?

Then read aloud Exodus 2:1-10. Discuss:

- How did Moses survive the killing of the Hebrew baby boys?
- What do these verses tell us about God?

Brainstorm a list of popular heroes from literature, movies, or comics who have well-known origin stories. (For example: We know that Superman and Supergirl were sent to earth to escape the destruction of Krypton; Luke Skywalker and Princess Leia were twins separated at birth.) List these heroes on a markerboard or large sheet of paper.

Look over your list of heroes and identify similarities between their origin stories and Moses' origin story. (For instance: Many heroes were raised by someone other than their parents; many grew up in a culture where they didn't quite fit in.) Discuss:

- Why do you think heroes' stories have so many elements in common?
- What do these stories tell us about things we look for or expect in our heroes?
- What does the story of Moses' birth and early life tell us about Moses and what we can expect from him?

Midwives to the Rescue (5 minutes)

Supplies: Bibles

Before Pharaoh ordered all the Hebrew baby boys thrown into the river, he had another plan. Read aloud Exodus 1:15-21. (Note: A midwife is a person who delivers babies.) Discuss:

- What instructions does Pharaoh give the midwives?
- What did the midwives do in response to these instructions?

Shiphrah and Puah, the midwives, were dishonest with Pharaoh when they told him that Hebrew women were so strong that they gave birth to babies before the midwives could get to them. Scripture tells us that God blessed them because of what they did to protect the Hebrew babies. Discuss:

- Do you think that Shiphrah and Puah were right to lie to Pharaoh? Why or why not?

Read Exodus 20:16. This command not to testify falsely or bear false witness, which God did not give to the Israelites until many years after Shiphrah and Puah lied to Pharaoh, is often interpreted as "Do not lie." Discuss:

- Would you say that lying is always wrong? Why or why not?
- In what situations, if any, might dishonesty be justified?
- How would things have happened differently if Shiphrah and Puah had been honest? Was there a way they could have been honest *and* saved the Hebrew babies?
- How did God respond to the midwives' actions? What, if anything, does this tell us about whether it's ever okay to be dishonest?

Closing Activity: Where Was God? (10 minutes)

Supplies: a candle that can easily be passed from one person to another

Often in the Bible's opening books we see God intervene directly in the lives of God's people. God speaks directly to leaders to give them instructions and works miracles to save and protect—and even to punish—the people of

15

Israel. But in the Scripture passages we looked at for this session, God doesn't appear to be a major player. In the story of Joseph, which tells us how God's people ended up in Egypt, God never speaks directly to Joseph nor does God perform any supernatural feats. While we know that Shiphrah and Puah served God and that God rewarded them, God isn't even mentioned in the story of Moses' birth and rescue on the banks of the Nile.

Though we don't see miracles or read direct quotations from God in these Scripture passages, God is very much at work in them. Spend a minute reflecting on how God is present in the stories you studied as a part of this session. (For example, maybe you see God in the courage of Moses' mother or in the events that brought the people of Israel to Egypt.)

Gather in a circle and light a candle. (You will need a candle that can easily be passed from one person to another.) Pass the candle around the circle. When participants hold the candle, they should name one way they see God at work in the Scripture passages and stories you read and discussed during this session. It's fine if some examples are repeated.

After the candle has gone all the way around the circle, have one person hold the candle while the group closes in prayer. (Use the prayer below or one of your own.)

Closing Prayer

God, thank you for this time we've had together to learn about and reflect on the life of Moses and the story of God's people. Open our eyes so that we can see how you are at work in our lives and in the world around us, just as you were at work in the lives of the Israelites and Moses' family. Remind us of your presence when we encounter hardships and challenges. And give us the strength and courage this week to listen for your word and do your will in all circumstances. Amen.

2.

TWO MOMENTS THAT DEFINED THE MAN

It's common in movies to open with an event from the protagonist's childhood and then, in the next scene, to skip ahead to a time when he or she is a full-grown adult. The Book of Exodus does this with Moses. In Exodus 2:9, Moses is a baby; in Exodus 2:11, he is an adult. The only thing that verse 10 tells us about Moses' childhood is that his mother finished nursing him and that after he had grown up, Pharaoh's daughter formally adopted him.

Despite this lack of information, we can make some assumptions about Moses' youth. We can assume that, as the adopted son of a princess, he grew up in luxury, a part of the royal family. Exodus 2:11 tells us that Moses recognized a Hebrew (Israelite) man as "one of his own people." So we can assume that Moses knew he wasn't Egyptian by birth and that in fact he belonged to the nation that Pharaoh had oppressed and enslaved. Moses was in a unique situation. He was both an Israelite and an Egyptian; he belonged both to the oppressed and to the oppressor.

The Move to Midian

This tension between Egyptian and Hebrew came to a head when Moses, as an adult, "went out among his people and he saw their forced labor" (verse 11). This may have been the first time that Moses fully understood the oppression faced by the Israelites. He saw an Egyptian slavemaster beating a Hebrew slave. In his anger, Moses killed the Egyptian and buried him in the sand. Though Moses had checked to ensure there were no witnesses, word of the killing spread and got back to Pharaoh. Pharaoh planned to kill Moses, so Moses left Egypt.

Living as a fugitive, Moses ended up in Midian, a region in what is now western Saudi Arabia, across the Reed Sea from Egypt. In Midian, Moses got involved in another confrontation. While he was sitting by a well, seven young women came to the well to draw water for their father's sheep and goats. But a group of shepherds chased them away. As he had when he saw the Israelite slave being beaten, Moses acted to protect those who were being hurt. But unlike his confrontation with the Egyptian slavemaster, where his rage made him a murderer and a fugitive, Moses' run-in with the shepherds earned him the favor of the young sisters who'd come to the well, and of their family.

The young women's father, Reuel (also known as Jethro), welcomed Moses into the family's home, and Moses married one of the women, Zipporah. Moses, the Israelite who was raised an Egyptian and became a fugitive on the run from the Egyptian Pharaoh, found stability in a foreign land.

Instructions from the Burning Shrubbery

Moses had escaped Egypt and the double life he'd had to live there. He established a new life and settled down with his family. But God had other plans (as God often does). One day many years later, while Moses was taking care of the family flock, he saw a bush that "was in flames" but "didn't burn up" (Exodus 3:2). The voice of God called out to him from the bush. There was a new king in Egypt, but the people of Israel were still being oppressed. God wanted Moses to lead the Israelites out of slavery and oppression and into a new life in the land of their ancestors.

Moses was reluctant. Egypt was the last place he wanted to go. He was comfortable with his life in Midian, so Moses gave excuses. "What if they don't believe me or pay attention to me?" (Exodus 4:1). God gave Moses signs and wonders to perform that would serve as evidence that God had sent him.

Moses protested that he didn't speak well. God called Moses' brother Aaron, who spoke very well, to be a spokesperson. Moses, out of excuses, asked God to send someone else. But God insisted that Moses was the guy for the job.

A God of Discomfort and Disruption

Growing up as royalty in Egypt, Moses never could have predicted that he would live much of his adult life as a shepherd in Midian. Nor could he have imagined that the God of the Israelites would choose him to confront Pharaoh and lead the Israelites to freedom. While Moses' situation was extraordinary, most of us will find that life often doesn't work out the way we expect it to. And most of us, like Moses, will discover that comfort is not permanent. There will always be disruptions that challenge us and force us to change our plans or rethink our priorities.

One indisputable truth of Scripture is that our God is a God of discomfort and disruption. The work of God's kingdom is messy, and little is accomplished when people stick to what is easy and obvious. Answering God's call will require us to make sacrifices, to interact with people whom we might otherwise avoid, and to pay attention to situations we might otherwise ignore. Like Moses, we will be tempted to make excuses. But if we are faithful to God's call, we will change the world in incredible ways.

Session 2 Activities

Opening Activity: Surprise! Life Happened (5-10 minutes)

Think back to when you were in first or second grade. What hopes or expectations did you have for your life? What did you imagine your life would be like when you were in middle school or high school?

Take a few minutes to reflect on these questions. Then have each person in the group say what expectations he or she had for the future several years ago. After everyone has had a chance to share, discuss:

- How is your life different from what you thought it would be like when you were younger?
- What changes might you have been able to predict? What changes were complete surprises?

19

Life rarely works out exactly the way we want it to or expect it to. This was certainly true for Moses. The life he lived as an adult was a far cry from what he knew growing up as the adopted son of an Egyptian princess. It definitely wasn't the life he would have picked for himself. But it was the life that God had chosen for Moses; and it was a life that still has an impact on the world today.

Opening Prayer

Lord, during our time together, open our eyes to see the unexpected; open our minds to new ideas and challenges; and open our hearts that we can learn and grow together as we continue this study. Amen.

Whatcha Gonna Do? (15 minutes)

Supplies: paper and pens or pencils

Two confrontations forever changed Moses' life. The first occurred when he witnessed an Egyptian beating a Hebrew slave. He responded in anger, killing the Egyptian. Moses became a fugitive and fled to Midian. There he witnessed a group of shepherds harassing seven young women who'd come to a well to draw some water. He drove off the shepherds to protect the women and thus met his future wife. Though he responded differently to each incident, with much different results, in both cases he acted to protect those who were vulnerable.

Spend a few minutes in silence identifying situations when you became aware that someone was suffering or being oppressed. Jot these down for yourself on a sheet of paper in two columns:

- The first column should include people whom you have come into contact with who were suffering or oppressed in some manner. This could include people who were homeless, who had fled life-threatening situations in other countries, who were struggling with addiction, and so on.
- The second column should include people in other parts of the country or world whom you have read about or heard about but have not seen face-to-face. Focus on people who, like the ancient Israelites, are suffering at the hands of a violent or oppressive regime. This might include refugees, slaves, groups whose basic

rights have been taken away or compromised, people suffering religious persecution, and so on.

Then take five minutes to go through both lists, answering three questions about each person or group listed:

- What did I do? (What did you do when you passed the homeless person on the street or read about children working in sweatshops?)
- What could I have done? (What could you have done in the past when you encountered or learned about these people that you didn't do?)
- What can I do? (What can you do now, or in the near future, to respond to the needs and injustice you encountered or learned about?)

Following this five-minute period, invite participants to name one person or group from each of their lists and to say how they answered each of the three questions with regard to those persons or groups.

Commit to follow through on one of the things that you came up with in response to the question, "What can I do?" As a group, hold one another accountable to your commitments and check up on your progress during your next session.

On the Run (Optional, 10 minutes)

Supplies: paper and pens or pencils

Read aloud Exodus 2:11-22. In these verses, a lot happens to Moses in a very short period of time.

- Up to this point, Moses likely had been living comfortably as a part of the royal family. What events caused his life to change very quickly?
- What decisions did Moses make? Do you think that these were wise decisions? Why or why not?
- When has your life changed suddenly? What decisions did you have to make on the fly? (It's okay if you don't feel comfortable talking about these events.)
- Knowing what you know now, how might you have responded differently to these events?
- Regardless of your choices, how was God present and at work during the sudden and difficult changes in your life?

We don't have a lot of details about the life Moses was living in Egypt. Nor do we have a lot of details about the life he was living in Midian. Based on what little we know from Scripture and on what we can guess or assume, compare Moses' royal life in Egypt with his life in Midian.

Divide into groups of three or four. Each group should fold in half a sheet of paper. Groups should title one half "Life in Egypt" and the other "Life in Midian." Then they should list examples of what they imagine Moses' life to have been like during his time in each of these places. Each example under "Life in Egypt" should have a corresponding example under "Life in Midian." For instance, if a group writes "Lived in the palace as part of the royal family" in the Egypt column, the group might write "Lived in a house with all of his in-laws" in the Midian column.

Spend a few minutes coming up with comparisons between Moses' life in Egypt and Midian. Then allow each group to read aloud a few of its examples. Discuss:

- How might running away to Midian have changed Moses' life for the better?
- What regrets might Moses have had about running away to Midian?

Answer the Burning Bush: Pros and Cons (10 minutes)

Supplies: Bibles, a markerboard or large sheet of paper, markers

Moses' life in Midian was different from what he'd grown up with in the house of the royal family. But he had a family in Midian, and he had safety and stability. This wouldn't last.

Read aloud Exodus 3:1-12. Discuss:

- What did you know about the story of Moses and the burning bush?
- What did you learn or notice about this story that you didn't know before?
- Why do you think God chose this method to get Moses' attention?
- What job did God offer Moses? How did God "pitch" this job to Moses?
- How did Moses respond to God's offer? What do you think Moses might have been thinking?

Often when people make a big life decision, such as a decision about whether to accept a job, they make a list of pros and cons—reasons for or against deciding a certain way.

Work together as a group to create a list of pros and cons for the job that God offered Moses. A pro might be "The opportunity to make a difference." A con might be "No experience negotiating with monarchs." Write these pros and cons on a markerboard or large sheet of paper.

After a few minutes, look over the list you've created. Discuss:

- Based on your list, what decision do you think Moses should have made?
- What factors do you think were most important to his decision?
- When have you wrestled with a tough decision? What factors did you have to weigh?
- How did God factor into your decision?

What's Your Excuse? (10 minutes)

Supplies: Bibles, scrap paper

Skim through Exodus 4:1-17, paying attention to excuses that Moses made to avoid answering God's call to go before Pharaoh and demand release of the Hebrew captives. Discuss:

- What did Moses say in response to God's request?
- What excuse(s) did Moses offer God?
- How did God respond?

Mentally or on a sheet of scrap paper make a list of situations in which someone asked you to do something you didn't want to do or felt ill-prepared to do. Once you've come up with a few examples, identify one situation in which you tried to avoid the thing you had been asked to do.

Then divide into pairs or groups of three. Pairs or groups should talk about the situations each person picked and the excuses each person came up with. Talk about whether each excuse or reason to say no was legitimate (and whether it was effective). As time permits, discuss whether there are situations when making excuses is justified.

Then, as time permits, play a little game. Before the session come up with many common tasks (at least one task for each participant) and write each task on a separate slip of paper. These might include doing homework, doing dishes, taking out the trash, and cleaning your room. Place the slips of paper in a hat or container. One at a time, participants should draw a slip from the container, read aloud the task written on it, and come up with an excuse for not doing that task.

Following this activity, discuss:

- What sorts of things has God called you to do? (These do not need to be examples where God spoke to you audibly or through incredible signs such as burning bushes; they can be examples where you felt compelled to do something, where a particular Scripture verse or passage stood out to you, or where you were offered an unexpected opportunity.)
- Have you ever felt a call to do something that made you uncomfortable? How did you respond?
- What excuses have you come up with to avoid something that you felt God was calling you to do?

Answering God's call is rarely easy. Often doing so requires discomfort or sacrifice. But we know from the example of Moses and others that the impact of answering God's call is more than worth the pain and hardship.

Closing Activity: Where Was God? (10 minutes)

Supplies: a candle that can easily be passed from one person to another

As you did in the first session, gather in a circle and light a candle. Pass the candle around the circle. When people have the candle, they should name one way they see God at work in Scripture and in the stories you read and discussed. It's okay if some examples are repeated.

After the candle has gone all the way around the circle, have one person hold the candle while the group closes in prayer. (Use the prayer below or one of your own.)

Closing Prayer

God of discomfort and disruption, thank you for this time we've had to reflect on the challenges and changes that defined Moses' life. We see in his example how you can use difficult and unforeseen circumstances to change the world. Give us the courage to answer your call and to make the sacrifices you ask of us, so that we can bring your love and grace to all whom we encounter. Amen.

3.

THE EXODUS

The villain in the story of Moses and the Israelites in Egypt is Pharaoh. The word *pharaoh* means "king," and the pharaoh who ordered the killing of the Hebrew baby boys at the beginning of Exodus is not the same pharaoh whom Moses confronted later in the book. Neither of these Egyptian kings is named in Scripture, and we don't have much in the way of historical and archaeological evidence to help us match the kings to the story.

Traditionally the pharaoh whom Moses confronted is identified as Ramesses II. Ramesses II, also known as Ramesses the Great, ruled for sixty-five years in the thirteenth century B.C. Though the Great Pyramids had been constructed many centuries earlier, Ramesses was responsible for many major building projects, including large statues of himself. (You can still see Ramesses' mummified remains at the Egyptian Museum in Cairo.)

When God called Moses, Moses was a shepherd who'd fled Egypt as a fugitive years earlier. Moses' task was to confront Ramesses, the ruler of the region's most powerful nation who was revered as a god (and saw himself as such).

One Stubborn Pharaoh

Moses' first attempt to convince Pharaoh to free the Israelites was a failure. Moses, with his brother Aaron, requested that the people be released from their work to celebrate a festival for God in the desert. Pharaoh, offended by the request, decided that the Israelites were not working hard enough. The slaves had been making bricks from mud and straw, which the pharaoh provided; now Pharaoh demanded that they gather their own straw but produce the same number of bricks.

Moses and Aaron went before Pharaoh again, this time demonstrating God's power by turning Aaron's staff into a snake. Pharaoh's court magicians were able to do the same thing (even though Aaron's snake devoured the magicians' snakes), so Pharaoh wasn't impressed and didn't budge.

God responded to Pharaoh's stubbornness with a series of plagues or disasters. God turned the Nile River to blood; sent armies of frogs and swarms of flies; struck the Egyptian people with sores; and killed off livestock. None of these plagues changed Pharaoh's mind. Each time, Pharaoh remained stubborn. And the Israelites remained as slaves in Egypt.

Triumph Through Tragedy

There were ten plagues in all, and the final plague involved the death of the firstborn son of every Egyptian family (human and livestock). This grim episode was the inspiration for the most important religious festival in ancient Israel and throughout the history of Judaism: the Passover. *Passover* refers to the angel of death passing over the Israelite households during the final plague. Following the plague of the firstborn and the Passover, Pharaoh relented, freed the Hebrew slaves, and allowed them to leave Egypt.

Then he changed his mind again. He sent his army after the Israelites. The Egyptian army met the Israelites as they neared the sea. Seeing the army, the people of Israel questioned Moses' leadership and asked him: Why did you lead us out of slavery just to have the Egyptians trap us and kill us in the desert? But God provided a way forward, by enabling Moses to part the waters so that the Israelites could cross the sea on dry land. When the Egyptian army followed, the waters closed on them, forever separating the Israelites from their oppressors.

God gave the people of Israel specific instructions for commemorating these events, instructions that Jewish people still today follow when they celebrate the Passover each spring.

The Ongoing Work of Freedom and Justice

Though the Passover has become the greatest Jewish celebration, the first Passover was a grim occasion. The Israelites had spent years in slavery, forced into hard labor and abused by their slavemasters. A series of plagues ravaged the people, land, and animals of Egypt. The firstborn son of every Egyptian family died as punishment for the cruelty of their leaders. And the Egyptian army drowned in the sea after being ordered to chase down the Israelites. But amid all the death and tragedy, God was liberating and nurturing an oppressed people.

Throughout Scripture, God takes an interest in people who are hurting and powerless. Those who are suffering or overlooked are still a priority for God today. God calls us to participate in the work of hope and freedom. This happens at the local level in our schools and communities when we pay attention and reach out to those who are ignored or suffering. It also happens on a global level as we participate in efforts to free those who are enslaved and to reach out to other victims of injustice.

Session 3 Activities

Opening Activity: What Will You Leave Behind? (5 minutes)

Scripture doesn't identify by name the pharaoh who was in power when Moses went back to Egypt to free the slaves, but Christians traditionally—based on biblical and historical evidence—have identified this pharaoh as Ramesses II. Ramesses reigned during a time of prosperity in Egypt. He oversaw massive building projects that asserted Egypt's dominance, and he went to great lengths to celebrate himself and his rule. Still today in Egypt you can see many statues of Ramesses II. You can even see Ramesses himself, as his mummy resides in the Egyptian Museum in Cairo.

Moses, on the other hand, left behind no artifacts that we know of. While Moses was a great leader, the people he led didn't build statues of him, nor did they revere him like a god. Discuss:

- What does it mean to leave behind a legacy? (*Legacy* might be defined as what one leaves behind after he or she dies.)
- What sort of legacy would you like to leave behind?
- How can your legacy point people not to you but to Christ?

Opening Prayer

Lord, guide us as we continue our journey with Moses and the Israelites. Show us the many ways that you're at work in these ancient stories and that you continue this work of freedom and liberation today. Amen.

Classic Mismatch (10 minutes)

Supplies: Bibles, paper, pens or pencils

Divide into groups of three or four. Each group should brainstorm a list of mismatches—competitions in which one person, team, or group has a substantial advantage over another in terms of size, strength, resources, or experience. After a couple minutes, have each group name some of its mismatches. Then discuss:

- What makes something a mismatch?
- When have you seen an underdog (the competitor at a disadvantage in a mismatch) pull out an unexpected victory against its opponent?
- How did the underdogs overcome the odds in these situations? What qualities does an underdog need in order to prevail in a mismatch?

Moses' confrontation with Pharaoh is on a level with any of history's great mismatches. Moses was eighty years old when he returned to Egypt in hopes of freeing the Israelites. Moses' brother Aaron, who served as his spokesman, was even older (Exodus 7:7). Pharaoh had the entire wealth, resources, and military strength of one of the world's most powerful empires. Moses didn't even have a relationship with the Israelite slaves whom he was representing.

Read aloud Exodus 5. (Break it up into chunks with a different person reading each paragraph or every few verses.) Discuss:

- What did Moses and Aaron ask for when they came before Pharaoh the first time?
- How did Pharaoh respond? What happened to the Israelites as a result?

- How did the Israelites react toward Moses and Aaron?
- How do you think this experience affected Moses and Aaron? How might it have affected their relationship with God?

Plagued (10-15 minutes)

Supplies: prepared cards with names of plagues

Moses and Aaron's first meeting with Pharaoh didn't go very well. Not only did Pharaoh refuse to meet their demands, but he also made life for the Israelites much more difficult. This episode had a negative impact on the people's confidence in Moses and Aaron and made the possibility of success seem very unlikely. But God wasn't finished with Moses and Aaron, or with Pharaoh.

God used a series of ten plagues to convince Pharaoh to free the Israelites. Discuss:

- What do you know about the plagues of Egypt?
- What would you like to know about the plagues?

(The purpose of the first question is just to get a sense of what people may know already. It's okay if participants don't have any familiarity with the plagues.)

Before the session, write down the following plagues, each on a separate index card or small square of paper:

- Plague of locusts
- Plague of frogs
- Plague of mold
- Plague of blood
- Plague of dust
- Plague of darkness
- Plague of hail and thunder
- Plague of heat
- Plague of lice
- Plague of boils or sores
- Plague of rats

- Plague of insects or flies
- Plague of ice
- Plague of the death of the firstborn
- Plague of diseased livestock

There are fifteen plagues listed. Your challenge (as a group) is twofold:

- Identify which ten plagues are the plagues listed in the Bible.
- Place the ten plagues in the order they occurred, from first to tenth.

Some readers have noticed that the ten plagues seem to build on one another. The bloody appearance of the Nile River water may have been the result of a red algae infestation that made the river toxic, driving the frogs onto the land and killing the fish, attracting gnats and flies, which carried disease to the livestock and to the people, and so on.

You may look at another interpretation of the plagues below (under "Matching, with Mythology"). But regardless of how we understand the meaning of the plagues and their progression, they serve as a testament to God's power and God's commitment to liberation. (For answers, see bottom of page.)

Matching, with Mythology (Optional, 5-10 minutes)

While some readers see a logical progression in the plagues, and some critical readers have come up with natural explanations for each plague, other readers see in the plagues a divine battle. Christian and Jewish readers see the plagues as God's method of influencing and punishing the Egyptians and their leaders. But there may be more at play. The instruments of the plagues—water, frogs, and so on—may have been statements against certain Egyptian gods. One Egyptian god was a water bearer, one had the head of a frog, one had the head of a fly, and so on.

"Plagued" answers (in this order): 1. Plague of blood, 2. Plague of frogs, 3. Plague of lice, 4. Plague of insects or flies, 5. Plague of diseased livestock, 6. Plague of boils or sores, 7. Plague of hail and thunder, 8. Plague of locusts, 9. Plague of darkness, 10. Plague of the death of the firstborn

If time permits, using the Internet or other sources, see if you can match each of the Egyptian deities to its plague-related occupation or appearance. (For answers, see bottom of page.)

Gods:

1. Geb
2. Hapi
3. Hathor
4. Heket
5. Isis
6. Khepri
7. Nut
8. Ra
9. Seth

Relationship to Plague:

a. God of the Nile, the river turned to blood (first plague)
b. Goddess of fertility, with the head of a frog (second plague)
c. God of the earth, whose dust gave way to lice (third plague)
d. God of creation, with the head of a fly (fourth plague)
e. Goddess of love and protection, with the head of a cow (fifth plague)
f. Goddess of medicine, such as that which would soothe boils or sores (sixth plague)
g. Goddess of the sky, where hail and thunder come from (seventh plague)
h. God of storms and disorder, such as an infestation of locusts (eighth plague)
i. God of the sun, which was overcome by darkness (ninth plague)

Discuss:

- What might this relationship between the plagues and the Egyptian gods tell us about God?
- What might it tell us about the Egyptian gods?

"*Matching with Mythology*" *answers (in this order):*
1.c, 2.a, 3.e, 4.b, 5.f, 6.d, 7.g, 8.i, 9.h

A Grim Cause for Celebration (Optional, 10 minutes)

Supplies: Bibles, a markerboard or large sheet of paper, markers

Discuss:

- What do you know about the Jewish festival of the Passover?
- Do you have Jewish friends who celebrate the Passover? If so, what have they told you about its meaning and importance?
- Have you taken part in a Passover Seder meal? If so, what do you remember about it? What did it teach you about Jewish tradition and belief?

Passover is the biggest celebration on the Jewish calendar, but the event that it commemorates is rather grim. Read aloud Exodus 12:1-13. Discuss:

- What did the tenth and final plague involve?
- What instructions did God give to the Israelites in preparation for this plague?
- Where does the name "Passover" come from?

As a group, make a list on a markerboard or large sheet of paper of all the elements included in the Passover celebration that are mentioned in Exodus 12. (Go beyond verse 13 to identify elements from later in the chapter.) After you've completed your list, discuss:

- Why do you think God instructed the Israelites to prepare for and commemorate the Passover with such an elaborate and particular ritual?

Escape to Freedom (5-15 minutes)

Supplies: Bibles

Discuss:

- What do you know about the story of the Israelites crossing the sea on dry land?

Read Exodus 14:1-31. Because this is a lengthy Scripture passage, have a different volunteer read aloud every few verses or one paragraph. Discuss:

- What did you learn from this Scripture passage that you didn't know before?
- In verse 4, God decides to "make Pharaoh stubborn" so that he would chase the Israelites. Why do you think God made Pharaoh act in this way?
- How did the Israelites respond as they approached the sea and saw the Egyptian army coming after them? Do you think their response was justified? Why or why not?

After the Israelites passed through the sea they were finally free from their oppressors, and they celebrated. Exodus 15:1-21 includes two Israelite victory songs. As time permits, divide into teams of three or four and do one of the following:

Option 1

Take the song of Moses (verses 1-18) or the much shorter song of Miriam (verse 21) and set it to a tune. As needed, make small changes to the wording to better fit the tune.

Option 2

Come up with a simple song of your own to commemorate the Israelites' escape to freedom.

Spend about five minutes working on your songs, and then allow each team to present what it came up with.

Justice and Mercy (5-10 minutes)

Supplies: Bibles

The Passover festival has been the biggest annual celebration for the Israelite and Jewish people for thousands of years. It commemorates an event in which God delivered God's people from years of slavery and oppression. But it also recalls an event that saw the death of the firstborn son in every Egyptian household and the drowning of the Egyptian army in the sea.

33

Read Exodus 12:29-32. Discuss:

- Christians believe that God is all-loving and full of grace. How do we square our belief in a loving God with the deaths of so many Egyptian children?
- What was the purpose behind the death of the firstborn (and all the other plagues)? In your opinion, does the purpose justify the killing of the Egyptian firstborn? Explain.
- Why do you think God's plague killed the firstborn sons instead of the Egyptian leaders and slavemasters themselves?
- Read Exodus 1:8-22. How do Pharaoh's earlier decisions to force the Hebrews into hard labor and to massacre Hebrew baby boys affect your thoughts about the death of the Egyptian firstborn?

You likely won't have time to resolve the questions of why God uses certain punishments and whether certain actions are consistent with God's love and grace. People of faith have struggled with these issues for centuries. Regardless of where we stand on these questions, Christians can affirm that (a) God is a God of both justice and mercy and (b) God ultimately carried out a plan of salvation for all people, regardless of nationality or position.

Closing Activity: Make a Commitment (10-15 minutes)

Supplies: a candle that can easily be passed from one person to another

Spend a few minutes in quiet reflection, thinking about one way you can reach out to people who are hurting and oppressed in your community. Think of something that is simple and that you can do in the next couple weeks. If possible, identify something you can do through your congregation's ministries.

As time permits, consider how you might also participate in God's work of freedom elsewhere in the world. A good place to start is the International Justice Mission, which is devoted to eliminating slavery and human trafficking around the globe. You can visit the International Justice Mission's website at www.ijm.org.

As you did in previous sessions, gather in a circle and light a candle. Pass the candle around the circle. When people hold the candle, they should name one way they see God at work in the Scriptures and stories that the group read and discussed. It's okay if some examples are repeated.

After the candle has gone all the way around the circle, have one person hold the candle while the group closes in prayer. (Use the prayer below or one of your own.)

Closing Prayer

God of freedom, thank you again for this opportunity to come together and study the story of your people. Open our eyes so we can recognize those in our world who are oppressed and enslaved and so we can see how you are doing the work of liberation. Give us the courage to join in your work of freedom. Amen.

4.

THE TEN COMMANDMENTS

Few passages of Scripture are as famous as Exodus 20:1-17, better known as the Ten Commandments. The Ten Commandments are the first of 613 laws God gave to Moses on Mount Sinai, which is also known as Mount Horeb.

The Israelites escaped from Egypt through the Reed Sea, which is likely one of the lakes between the Mediterranean Sea to the north and the Red Sea to the south that in modern times have been bisected by the Suez Canal. They then made their way into the desert of the Sinai Peninsula. After a three-month journey, they set up camp at the base of Mount Sinai. God came to rest on the mountain, which was smoking because "the LORD had come down on it with lightning" (Exodus 19:18). God called on Moses to come to the top of the mountain, but the rest of the Israelites had to keep their distance.

While Moses was on top of the mountain, God gave him the set of laws that we know as the Ten Commandments, along with other rules and instructions. But these ten were especially important, and the tablets on which they were written were contained in the ark of the covenant, the vessel that went before the Israelite army in battle and that would eventually reside in the inner chamber of the Temple in Jerusalem.

These Ten Commandments spoke to the people's relationship with God and with one another. The first few commandments told the Israelites they were to have no other gods, that they were not to create and worship idols, that they were not to misuse God's name, and that they were to honor God by observing the Sabbath day. The remainder of the commandments told God's people to honor their parents and to avoid practices that would be hurtful to others and to the community as a whole.

Set Apart

Some of the commandments seem obvious and would probably be included in any list of rules or laws. Most people, regardless of their belief system, would agree that murder and stealing are wrong. Other commandments are more specific to God's people. Unlike many of their neighbors, the Israelites were not to serve multiple gods or to worship foreign gods, nor were they to represent God using images or symbols. God also commanded them to set aside the seventh day of each week as a day when they would do no work.

The commandment to rest on the Sabbath set God's people apart. It was a unique reminder of both their dependence on God and the story of creation. Yet this commandment, and with the instruction not to use God's name in vain, are the ones that God's people today are most likely to ignore or dismiss. Saying, "Oh, my G—," or doing homework on Sunday don't seem as serious to us as worshiping other gods or committing adultery. Yet these commandments were among those that God considered most crucial, and they're among the ways that God's people show the world who they are and whom they serve.

They're Still Important, All of Them

Regardless of whether a commandment seems obvious or out of place in today's world, we should prayerfully consider what it means to be faithful to that commandment in our lives. What idols or false gods compete for our attention? Few of us are tempted to worship Egyptian or Canaanite deities, but we might feel drawn to the gods of money or popularity (or even sports or grades). Even if we aren't guilty of murder in the legal sense, how might we be acting violently toward others through our words or actions?

The Ten Commandments were the first in a set of hundreds of rules that would define the Israelites as God's people. And they are still relevant for us, the Israelites' spiritual descendants, as we strive to serve God and live as a community of faith.

Session 4 Activities

Opening Activity: Can You Name All Ten? (10 minutes)

The list of Ten Commandments that God gave Moses is one of the most famous passages in the Bible. You can usually find a poster showing all the commandments somewhere in your church building (if not in multiple places). In recent years they've become the subject of controversy, as cities and towns have debated whether it's appropriate to display the Ten Commandments in public spaces.

While just about everyone knows *of* the Ten Commandments, far fewer people can name the commandments themselves. Do one of the following commandment-naming activities:

- See how many commandments you can name individually. Record the commandments you come up with on a sheet of scrap paper (or on the "notes" application of your electronic device).
- Divide into groups of three or four. Have each group work together to assemble a list of ten commandments. Every group needs to have exactly ten commandments on its list, even if group members aren't certain that some of the commandments are correct.

After participants or groups have had several minutes to work, check everyone's answers by looking at Exodus 20:1-17. (As needed, refer to "A Note on Commandment Numbering," on the next page.) Then discuss:

- How well did you do coming up with the commandments? Did you do better or worse than you'd expected?
- What surprised you when you looked at the actual commandments? What surprised you because it was on the list? What surprised you because it wasn't?

- Why do you think the Ten Commandments have such a prominent place in our culture?
- Which of the commandments have become part of our laws and customs?
- Which of the commandments do we not take seriously, or even ignore?

Opening Prayer

God of justice and guidance, thank you for this time we have together. Watch over us as we study your laws and discuss what it means to live as your people. Amen.

A Note on Commandment Numbering

While just about everyone knows that the Bible contains a list of ten commandments, Scripture itself doesn't number them. And if you were to read Exodus 20, numbering as you go, you might come up with only nine.

Many Protestant churches traditionally have identified two separate commandments in Exodus 20:3-6, the first being, "You must have no other gods before me," and the second being, "Do not make an idol for yourself." For these Protestants, these are the first two commandments.

However, Roman Catholics, for example, traditionally see Exodus 20:3-6 as a single commandment: not making idols is part of having no other gods. This would leave Catholics short one commandment, but while many Protestants consider Exodus 20:17 ("Do not desire" or "covet") a single commandment, it is considered by some churches, including Roman Catholic, as two: not desiring a neighbor's wife is separate from not coveting a neighbor's property.

Jewish readers consider *both* Exodus 20:3-6 *and* Exodus 20:17 to be single commandments. But Jewish tradition numbers "You must have no other gods before me" as the second commandment. The first comes from Exodus 20:2: "I am the LORD your God who brought you out of Egypt."

Graven Images (10 minutes)

Supplies: Bibles

Read Exodus 20:1-6. Some readers consider these verses a single commandment; others see as many as three commandments at play; some traditionally identify two. At any rate, the meaning behind these opening verses is clear: the Israelites are to have a relationship with God alone and reject any deities that might compete for their allegiance.

Scripture specifically mentions creating idols. Often when we think of idols, we think of little statues representing divine beings that are worshiped by pagan religions. We think of them as artifacts from another era. (Or we use the word *idol* to describe celebrities with an obsessive fan base.) But idols are still a reality in our culture today. We can define an idol as anything that might take priority over God in our lives, regardless of whether it takes the form of a statue that we might find in a temple.

Work together to brainstorm a list of idols that people in our culture revere or worship. This could include tangible things such as electronics or homes; it also could include abstract concepts such as popularity or influence.

Spend about two minutes brainstorming. Then go through the items on your list and discuss how each might become an idol: How might it interfere with a person's relationship with God? Then discuss:

- Which of these idols have you struggled with?
- When have you put some of these things before God—or before friends or family or church?
- What makes these idols so tempting?
- What steps can you take to avoid making these idols a priority?

The Two We Like to Skip (10 minutes)

Supplies: Bibles

Look over the Ten Commandments in Exodus 20:1-17. Discuss:

- Which of these commandments, being completely honest with yourself, are you least likely to obey?

While answers to this question will vary, two of the commandments that our culture tends to disregard are the commandments not to misuse the Lord's name and to treat the Sabbath day as holy.

Read Exodus 20:7-11, if possible from various translations. Discuss:

- What does it mean to misuse God's name, use God's name in vain, or use "God's name as if it were of no significance"?
- What does it mean to keep the Sabbath day holy? What instructions does Scripture offer for observing the Sabbath?

Divide into groups of three or four. In these groups, discuss your feelings toward these two commandments. Consider some of the following questions:

- How hard do you try to avoid saying, "Oh, my G___," or using "Jesus Christ" as an expletive?
- What are some other ways that people misuse God's name?
- How important to you is refraining from work on Sundays?
- What are some other ways that people can honor—or dishonor— the Sabbath day?

After a few minutes of discussion, consider the following:

The commandment against using "God's name as if it were of no significance" or taking God's name "in vain" certainly includes flippantly saying God's name ("Oh, my G___"), but it also includes using God's name for selfish purposes. Often people of faith are quick to say that God supports our particular point of view, without prayerfully considering God's truth and priorities. Discuss:

- Aside from saying things such as "Oh, my G___," what are some ways that people misuse God's name?
- How might these ways be harmful?

Exodus 20:8-11 instructs God's people (along with their servants and livestock) to refrain from doing any work on the Sabbath day. Christians traditionally regard Sunday as the Sabbath day. (For Jewish people, the Sabbath is from sundown Friday to sundown Saturday.) Requiring people to take a day off may seem like an odd commandment, especially when it is included on a list with not killing and not worshiping false gods. But time for rest and renewal is essential. Without time for rest, our quality of work tends to suffer, as does our physical and mental health. Sabbath rest also gives us time and space for worship and to reflect on our priorities and relationship with God. Discuss:

- In your opinion, what is the importance of Sabbath rest? Why does God make it such a priority?
- What reasons might people give for not honoring the Sabbath or making time for rest?
- What are the values and benefits of rest? What aspects of your life (quality of work, attitude, relationships, and so on) suffer when you don't get enough rest?
- Read Mark 2:23-28. What do Jesus' words in these verses tell us about the Sabbath? What does it mean for the Sabbath to have been "created for humans"? How is the Sabbath a gift?

Honor Your Parents (5 minutes)

Supplies: Bibles, paper or note cards, pens or pencils

Most of the commandments deal either with the people's relationship with God (not making idols, not misusing God's name, and so on) or the people's relationship with the larger community (not killing or stealing). But one commandment deals specifically with the people's relationships with their parents: "Honor your father and your mother so that your life will be long on the fertile land that the LORD your God is giving you" (Exodus 20:12).

Paul, in the New Testament, actually refers to this commandment. Read Ephesians 6:1-4. Discuss:

- What does Paul have to say about this commandment?
- What do you think is the meaning of the promise in Exodus "so that your life will be long" or "so that things will go well for you"?
- Parents are not perfect; some parents act in ways that are hurtful to their children. What does it mean to "honor" parents who are in the wrong?

In the spirit of this commandment, write a note honoring your parent(s). "Parent" for the purposes of this activity may refer to any adult who has taken on a parental role in your life—anyone whom you would call "mother," "father," or "like a mother" or "like a father." This note should honor your parent(s) by describing reasons why you appreciate them and what they do. Find an appropriate time to give this note to your parent(s)—whether the next time you see them, when you reach a major milestone, when you graduate from high school, or at some other time.

More Than Just Killing and Cheating (5 minutes)

Supplies: Bibles

Reread Exodus 20:13-14. These commandments may seem obvious. Most people can agree that murder and cheating on a spouse are wrong. But there's more to these commandments than what is on the surface. Jesus mentioned these two commands in his Sermon on the Mount in the New Testament.

Read Matthew 5:21-30. Then discuss:

- What does Jesus teach about murder?
- How does Jesus expand our understanding of murder? Why do you think he equates rage and name-calling with murder?
- What does Jesus teach about adultery?
- How does Jesus expand our understanding of adultery? What do you think he means by cutting out our eyes or cutting off our hands if they cause us to sin?

Lying, Cheating, and Stealing (Optional, 10 minutes)

Supplies: Bibles, prepared index cards

Read aloud Exodus 20:15-16. Discuss:

- What does it mean to "testify falsely" or "bear false witness"?
- Why do you think Scripture says "testify falsely" or "bear false witness" instead of "lie"?

Write each of the items below on a separate index card or small sheet of paper. (If your group is especially large, make multiple card sets—one for every four or five people.) Work together to sort the cards into three categories:

Category 1

Things that are okay, no matter what.

Category 2

Things that are technically wrong, but aren't really a big deal.

Category 3

Things that are wrong, no matter what.

If there is a dispute about where to put a particular item, go with the majority opinion. The items are as follows:

- Copying another student's homework assignment
- Watching a newly released movie online through an illegal torrent site
- Spreading gossip about a peer that may or may not be true
- Lying to friends to spare their feelings
- Borrowing an article of clothing from a sibling without asking
- Illegally downloading an album without paying for it
- Copying from another student on a major test
- Not telling a cashier that he or she gave you too much change

The Things We Covet (Optional, 5 minutes)

Supplies: Bibles

Read aloud Exodus 20:17. Go around the room and invite participants to name one thing they would really like to have. After everyone has said something, discuss:

- Which of the items mentioned are most attainable? (In other words, who is most likely one day to get the desired item?)
- Which of the items mentioned are least attainable? (In other words, who is least likely one day to get the desired item?)
- What does it mean to "covet" something? (A simple definition of covet is "a desire to have something." You might refer to online dictionaries for additional definitions.)
- Why do you think God includes not coveting among the Ten Commandments?

- How can coveting—particularly a neighbor's belongings or relationships—be destructive? How can coveting hurt our relationships with God and others?

Closing Activity: What's Next? (10 minutes)

Supplies: a candle that can easily be passed from one person to another

As you did in previous sessions, gather in a circle and light a candle. Pass the candle around the circle. When people have the candle, they should name one way they will apply what they have learned from the Ten Commandments in the coming week. Consider:

- Which commandments do you think about differently as a result of this session?
- Which commandments do you understand better or take more seriously as a result of this session?

After the candle has gone all the way around the circle, have one person hold the candle while the group closes in prayer. (Use the prayer below or one of your own.)

Closing Prayer

God of justice and guidance, thank you for bringing us together to study your law. Show us how we can apply our new knowledge and understanding of your commandments to the decisions we make each day. Give us the wisdom to see how being faithful to your commandments will improve our relationships with you and with one another. Amen.

5.

LESSONS FROM THE WILDERNESS

Moses was an Israelite by birth, but there was always distance between him and the people he led. He grew up as part of the Egyptian royal family, while the rest of the Israelites were in slavery. When as an adult Moses became aware of the hardships the other Israelites faced, he left for Midian and started a family in another country. When the Israelites camped out at Mount Sinai, Moses withdrew from the camp for days at a time to meet privately with God.

While Moses had help from his brother, Aaron, and his sister, Miriam, he was mostly a one-man show. He spoke to God on behalf of the people, led them against threatening nations such as the Amalekites (Exodus 17:8-16), listened to the people's complaints when they were tired and hungry, taught "God's regulations and instructions" (18:16), and sat as judge for every conflict the people brought to him. The Bible suggests that the Israelites numbered in the millions during their time in the wilderness. While we don't have archaeological evidence to back this up, we can safely assume that Moses was dealing with a lot of people.

Wisdom from the In-Laws

Conflicts with in-laws have been a plot device on dozens of television comedies. If our knowledge of American culture came only from old sitcoms, we might assume that getting into petty disputes with our spouse's parents is an important part of being a married person in America. But despite what reruns on cable teach us, many people have great relationships with their in-laws. Moses was one such person.

A couple of months into the Israelites' trek through the desert, Moses got a visit from his father-in-law, Jethro (known elsewhere as Reuel). Jethro noticed that Moses was working nonstop and was at risk of burning out. Perhaps Jethro felt that his daughter deserved better than to be married to a workaholic who had no time for family. Regardless, he had a heart-to-heart conversation with his son-in-law and suggested that Moses appoint judges who would do the daily work of managing minor legal matters. Moses took Jethro's advice and delegated responsibility to "capable persons from all Israel" (18:25).

Grumble, Grumble

Appointing judges lightened Moses' workload, but it didn't solve all his problems. Throughout their time in the wilderness, the people of Israel grumbled and complained about their situation. While modern readers sometimes look down on the Israelites for lacking faith, their frustration was understandable. They were traveling through a barren wilderness. Food and water weren't readily available. They didn't have maps and weren't entirely clear about where they were going or how they were getting there.

One early complaint involved the food situation. "The whole Israelite community" (Exodus 16:2) reminded Moses that as slaves in Egypt they always had had food to eat. And they accused Moses of bringing them into the wilderness to starve.

God didn't care for the people's attitude but nonetheless provided them with what they needed. When the only available water was bitter, God gave Moses a way to make it sweet. Later, when there was no water at all, God made water flow from a rock. God answered the people's cries for food with a flock of quail and with morning dew that turned into a mysterious flaky bread they called *manna*. Over and over again, God gave the Israelites what they needed. But conditions remained harsh, and each time the grumbling and complaining would resume.

Faith Over Fear

The Israelites' destination was the land that God had set aside for them in Canaan. God commanded Moses to send ahead spies from each of Israel's tribes to scout the land and learn about the vegetation, the land's fertility, and the people. The spies spent forty days in the Promised Land. When they returned, two of the spies—Caleb and Joshua—reported that the land was very good and that the Israelites were equipped to take possession of it. The other spies disagreed. They were intimidated by the people living in Canaan and were certain the Israelites would be destroyed. When the Israelites heard the spies' report, they erupted and demanded to return to Egypt.

Because of the people's fear and lack of faith, God decided that no adult Israelites—aside from Joshua and Caleb—would enter the Promised Land. The people would wander in the desert for the rest of their lives.* Then, after their deaths, their children would inherit what God had promised. (Read the whole story in Numbers 13–14.)

There are times in our lives when our complaints and frustrations are justified. There are times when our needs are not met—or are not met in the way we expect them to be. But even when we are hurting or lacking, we can't give in to fear and doubt. We need to open our eyes to see how God is present with us and where God is leading us. We need to remember that, even though the Israelites had decades of struggles in the desert, God never left them. And, through Christ and the Holy Spirit, God never leaves us.

---

* Adam Hamilton makes it clear in his book that the Israelites didn't really "wander": "When we speak of the forty-year 'wilderness wandering' of the Israelites, the phrase is a bit of misnomer. The Israelites, after leaving Egypt, traveled for three months to Mount Sinai and remained there eleven months. (By way of reminder, everything from Exodus 19 to Numbers 10:10 is set during the eleven months at Mount Sinai.) Then the Israelites left Mount Sinai and made their way to a place called Kadesh or Kadesh Barnea.... Depending upon the precise route the Israelites took from Mount Sinai to Kadesh Barnea, it would have taken less than a month to travel there. Following their arrival, the Israelites spent most of the next thirty-eight years camped at Kadesh Barnea. This means that of the forty years the Israelites spent in the wilderness, less than six months was spent 'wandering.' They spent eleven months at Mount Sinai and thirty-eight years at Kadesh Barnea, before moving on to Mount Nebo."

Session 5 Activities

Opening Activity: God Provides (10 minutes)

Supplies: Bibles

Discuss:

- What are some times in your life when, even though things seemed to be falling apart, everything somehow just worked out?

Read Matthew 6:25-34.

- What does Jesus say in these verses about how God provides for our needs?
- What does it mean for God to provide for us?
- In what ways do you think God has provided for you?

Though we affirm that God provides for us, we also know that many people suffer from hunger, sickness, and grief and that sometimes their suffering persists.

- If God is all-loving and promises to provide, why do people suffer from oppression, chronic illness, long-term hunger, and homelessness?
- How does God work through people to end suffering and meet needs?
- How might God use you to meet the needs of those who are suffering?

Opening Prayer

Lord, you were present with the ancient Israelites as they traveled through the wilderness, and you are present with us still today. Guide us during this time together as we learn about you and your people and as we struggle with difficult questions. Thank you for this opportunity to grow together in faith. Amen.

Delegate (10 minutes)

Supplies: Bibles, inexpensive building kits

Select four volunteers from your group. One of the four will work individually on this activity; the other three will work as a team. In the team, one of the three people should be designated as the leader. Give identical small building kits to both the individual and the team. These kits should include at least a few dozen pieces. (You likely can find inexpensive building kits at a dollar store.)

Allow both the individual and the team a minute to look over the instructions for the kit. During this time, the team should devise a plan for putting together the kit. This plan should involve the leader of the team assigning a role to each of the other people. The objective is to split up the work so that the team will be able to put together the kit more quickly. (If resources permit, have enough building kits for everyone to participate. Most participants will work as part of a team, but a few will work individually.)

After the preparation time, the individual and team will race to see who can put together the kit most quickly. Declare a winner. Then discuss:

- What advantage did the three-person team have in this situation? Were they able to use their advantage to win?
- What are some other activities for which working as a team or a group is more efficient than working alone?

Read Exodus 18:13-27. Discuss:

- What roles and responsibilities had Moses taken on?
- What advice did Moses get from his father-in-law, Jethro?
- When have you been reluctant to ask for help, even though your workload was difficult for you alone to handle?
- What does this Scripture passage teach us about leadership and responsibility?
- What lessons does this Scripture passage have for the church?
- What are the dangers of taking on too many responsibilities? How can it harm the person who is taking on too much? How can it harm other people?

Quit Your Whining (10 minutes)

Think of a recent time when you were particularly irritated and uncomfortable. This may have been an occasion when you spent several hours in the hot sun without much to drink or when you were stuck out in the cold and couldn't stay warm no matter what you tried or when you were on a long car trip and had to use the bathroom, but the next exit wasn't for miles. (Stick to examples of temporary discomfort, irritation, and frustration rather than examples of illness or tragedy.) As you talk about these incidents, discuss the following questions:

- How did your irritation or discomfort affect your mood? your attitude? your ability to be reasonable and rational?
- What kind of relief did you seek? How did the kind of relief that would be acceptable change over time? (For instance, when you first needed to use the restroom, you may have been willing to wait for a nice rest area or restaurant bathroom; as your need intensified, you might have been willing to settle for a dirty gas station bathroom—or even the side of the road.)
- How did you express your irritation or discomfort? How did the people around you respond?
- How did you feel when relief finally came? How did your mood and attitude change?

When we are hungry, tired, or thirsty, we lose patience, anger more easily, and become more vocal about our complaints. Following their escape from Egypt, the Israelites spent many years in the desert. They undoubtedly spent a lot of time hungry, thirsty, and tired. And they were in an environment that didn't offer much in the way of relief. When they were thirsty, they didn't know when they would next encounter water; when they were tired, they didn't know when they would have a place to rest.

Read Exodus 16:2-3. This is one of several examples from Scripture in which the Israelites groaned or complained about their situation. Discuss:

- What were the Israelites complaining about?
- Do you think that they were justified in their complaint? Why or why not?
- What did the Israelites say to Moses about their situation?

Imagine that you were Moses and were hearing the people's complaint. How would you respond? Think specifically about how you would assure them and give them hope and about how you would react when they asked to return to slavery in Egypt.

Pair off. One person in each pair should read what the Israelites said to Moses in Exodus 16:3. The other person should respond to this complaint as if he or she were Moses. Partners should switch roles and repeat the activity. Then discuss:

- How did it feel to have to respond to complaints?
- How can complaining about something be productive and effective? How can complaining become whining and make situations worse?

"What Is it?" "Exactly." (Optional, 5 minutes)

Supplies: Bibles

Moses had the unenviable job of responding to people who were hungry and tired and saw little hope for their future. But whenever the people groaned and grumbled, God had a response. Read Exodus 16:4-8, 13-15, 31. Discuss:

- How did God respond to the Israelites' complaints?
- What kind of food did God provide for the people?

Reread verses 15 and 31. The word *manna* essentially means "What is it?" and suggests that the Israelites found it unusual. This story reminds us that, while God hears our complaints and answers our prayers, God often responds in ways we don't expect.

- When has God met your needs in an unusual or surprising way?

The Buffet (10 minutes)

Supplies: Bibles, markerboard or large sheet of paper, markers, paper, pens or pencils

As a group, create an imaginary buffet with between twenty and thirty items. Have each participant come up with a certain number of buffet items.

(For instance, if you have eight participants, have each person come up with three items.) Try to ensure that you have a good mix of main dishes, sides, salads, soups, breads, and so forth. List the buffet items on a markerboard or large sheet of paper.

Once your buffet is complete, everybody should make a plate or plates. You can make a plate either by drawing a plate with buffet items on it or by making a list of all the buffet items you would choose. Where possible, you should specify quantities and amounts. (For example, "two rolls" or "two large scoops of banana pudding.") There is no limit to how many buffet items you can select or how much of a certain item you can put on a plate. If you plan to make multiple trips through the buffet, take this into account, drawing additional plates as necessary.

Allow volunteers to talk about which items they chose from the buffet. Then discuss:

- How did you decide which items and how much of each item to put on your plate?
- Was the amount of food selected more or less than what you would normally eat at a meal?
- Realistically, do you think that you would actually eat all the food on your plate? How much consideration did you give to not wasting food?
- When you actually eat at a buffet or a potluck dinner, do you tend to put a reasonable amount of food on your plate or do you take too much? How much consideration do you give to not wasting food?

When God offered manna to the hungry Israelites, the manna came with specific instructions: take only what you need. Taking only what we need is easy when resources are scarce and we have to scrape just to meet our needs. But when there's abundance—when there's enough for us to eat our fill then go back for seconds and thirds—having the resolve to take only what we need can be a challenge.

Read Exodus 16:16-26. Discuss:

- What instructions did God give the people regarding the manna God was providing for them?

- What happened when the Israelites took more than their portion of manna?
- How much thought do you give to the amount of food, water, electricity, fuel, and so on that you use? Which of these resources do you sometimes use carelessly?
- In addition to honoring the rules that God gave the Israelites in the wilderness, what reasons do we have for making wise and responsible use of resources and not wasting or overusing?
- How can we honor God through our decisions about how we use resources?
- How do our choices involving resources affect other people?

Suck It Up (Optional, 10 minutes)

Supplies: Bibles

Divide into teams of three or four. Discuss in your teams:

- When have you been terrified of something you felt you had to do?
- How did you respond? Did you come up with excuses to avoid going through with it? Did you build yourself up so that you would be able to go through with it?

Read the following summary of Numbers 13:25–14:25. If time permits, read the actual Scripture passage.

> About two years after the Israelites' escape from Egypt, Moses sent twelve spies (one from each of Israel's twelve tribes) into Canaan and the land that God had promised the Israelites. The spies reported that, while the land itself was very good, it was populated by large, powerful people and its cities had "huge fortifications" (13:28). Though a spy named Caleb insisted that the Israelites were equipped to enter the Promised Land and deal with its people, many of the other spies insisted that the Israelites would be destroyed.
>
> The people didn't think much of Caleb's optimism and gave in to fear. They lashed out at Moses and said that it would be better for them to return to Egypt. God responded by saying, "I'll strike [the Israelites] down with a plague and disown them" (14:12).

But Moses pleaded with God not to give up on the Israelites. God listened to Moses' pleas and changed the punishment: no adult Israelite, except for Caleb and another faithful spy named Joshua, would enter the Promised Land. Because the others gave in to fear, they would spend the rest of their lives in the wilderness and their children would inherit God's blessings.

Discuss:

- When has fear kept you from taking hold of an opportunity, trying something new, or standing up for something important?
- What are some consequences of giving in to fear?
- Where can we find strength and courage when fear tempts us?

Closing Activity: What Now? (10 minutes)

Supplies: a candle that can easily be passed from one person to another

As you did in previous sessions, gather in a circle and light a candle. Pass the candle around the circle. When people have the candle, they should name one way this lesson relates to their life today. Consider:

- How has God provided for your life in surprising ways?
- How has fear kept you from being the person God has called you to be?

After the candle has gone all the way around the circle, have one person hold the candle while the group closes in prayer. (Use the prayer below or one of your own.)

Closing Prayer

God our provider, thank you for your many blessings and promises. Thank you for being patient with us when we are tired and when we struggle with fears and doubts. Thank you for the strength and courage we need to be the people you call us to be. In the coming week, watch over us so that we can be faithful to your will and take hold of your blessings. Amen.

6.

DON'T FORGET...PASS IT ON

Moses, like many of the people he led, would not live in the Promised Land. He had given up a comfortable life in Midian to become the leader of the Israelites; he had confronted Pharaoh to win Israel's freedom; he had heard every complaint about food, water, and difficult conditions; and he was the one who had to answer to God whenever the people messed up.

But after all that and after forty years in the desert, Moses knew that he would die before the Israelites entered the Promised Land. This was due to one instance when Moses disobeyed God, striking a rock to produce water instead of speaking to it as God had instructed. In response, God had told Moses that because he had failed to trust God fully, he would not lead his people into their new home. (See Numbers 20:12.) While this likely was heartbreaking for Moses, he didn't let disappointment keep him from the important work that God had called him to do. So Moses prepared the Israelites for their future in the Promised Land, a future that would not include him.

For the Children

Shortly after the Israelites escaped from Egypt, God began preparing them for the future. God gave them instructions for celebrating annual festivals; God intended these celebrations to continue far into the future. Long before they entered the Promised Land, God also gave the Israelites detailed laws to govern how they would live when they got there. There are laws in the Book of Leviticus, for example, that deal with land ownership and people of other nations living in the Promised Land. The original plan was for the people receiving these laws and instructions to settle Israel's new home and establish a legal system. But after the adult Israelites were punished for their lack of faith and barred from entering the Promised Land, their role changed. They had to pass down God's law and wisdom to their children and grandchildren.

The most basic and essential law that the people were to teach their children was "Love the LORD your God with all your heart, all your being, and all your strength" (Deuteronomy 6:5). God, through Moses, instructed the Israelites to keep these words with them at all times: "Talk about them when you are sitting around your house and when you are out and about.... Tie them on your hand as a sign. They should be on your forehead as a symbol" (6:7-8). Younger Israelites—the ones who would grow up to settle the Promised Land—needed to understand their identity as God's people; they needed to know what set them apart.

The View from Mount Nebo

Before Moses died, God allowed him to walk to the top of Mount Nebo and look out on the land that his people would inhabit. Mount Nebo, which today is in Jordan, is not a large mountain. Its maximum elevation is less than three thousand feet. But it offers a panoramic view of the Promised Land in Israel. On Mount Nebo, Moses got a glimpse of the future—a future he had worked to build but would not be a part of.

As children of God and followers of Christ, we all work toward a future that God promises one day will not have sin and death, injustice and oppression. We see glimpses of this promised future wherever people are working to spread the love of Christ, to fight poverty and hunger, to show compassion to those who are sick or imprisoned, or to eliminate slavery and human trafficking. And we can show people, through our words, actions, and example, what this promised future will look like.

Session 6 Activities

Opening Activity: Don't Forget (5-10 minutes)

Supplies: Bibles, a markerboard or large sheet of paper, marker

Take a minute to brainstorm, individually, a list of things that you never forget to do. This could include things that you do every morning as you get ready for the day or every night as you prepare for bed. It could involve your routine at school or work that you do for an activity (such as a sport or an instrument). Record these things on a markerboard or large sheet of paper.

Allow volunteers to read aloud their lists. Then discuss:

- What is it about these things that makes them unforgettable?
- Have you ever forgotten one of these unforgettable things? If so, what circumstances caused you to forget?

Read Deuteronomy 6:1-9. Discuss:

- What does Moses want the Israelites to remember?
- What instructions does he give them to ensure that they don't forget?

Opening Prayer

Lord, bless our time together as we reflect on our place in God's story. As we grow together in faith, remind us how our actions have an impact on others, including those in future generations. Amen.

For the Next Generation (5-10 minutes)

Supplies: Bibles

Reread Deuteronomy 6:6-7. Moses didn't just want the people to remember this commandment for themselves. It was also important that they teach this commandment to their children.

- What would happen if the adult Israelites remembered and faithfully recited the commandment to love God with all their being but never bothered to teach the commandment to their children?

Scripture tells us that aside from Joshua and Caleb, none of the adult Israelites who left Egypt would be alive when God's people arrived in the Promised Land. Thus, while they were still alive it was essential that they pass along to their children the stories, the many commandments God had given them, and the instructions for their sacred festivals.

Divide into teams of three or four to discuss the following.

- In what ways have adults passed along their faith to you? Which of these ways do you think have been most effective?
- How do you pass along your faith to those younger than you? How do you do this through church activities? through family relationships? through example?
- What else can you do to pass along your knowledge and experience of Christ to younger children?

Allow three or four minutes for discussion. Then have each team summarize its discussion for the rest of the group. As a group, decide on two or three tangible ways that you can pass along your faith to those younger than you.

Variation on a Mezuzah (15 minutes)

Supplies: Bibles, paper, note cards, markers; other supplies are optional

Reread Deuteronomy 6:4-9. The commandment "Love the LORD your God with all your heart, all your being, and all your strength" is called the *Shema*, which is the Hebrew word for "listen" or "hear." Notice that verse 4 begins, "Israel, listen!"

These verses tell the Israelites to take the words of this commandment and tie them on their hands, place them on their foreheads, and write them on the doorframes of their homes. Some Jewish people still today take these instructions very literally.

Take a couple of minutes to use phones and other electronic devices to find images of *mezuzahs* and *tefillin*. These are devices that allow Jewish people to be faithful to God's words in Deuteronomy 6:8-9. *Mezuzahs* are small decorative boxes containing the *Shema* that people can affix to their doorframes. *Tefillin* are small leather boxes containing Scripture that people can tie to their wrists and foreheads.

Using common supplies such as paper, note cards, and markers or using an electronic device, come up with a reminder in the spirit of a *mezuzah* or *tefillin*. Whatever you create should use the words of Deuteronomy 6:5: "Love the LORD your God with all your heart, all your being, and all your strength." You might also include other verses or reminders of God's love and grace. Here are some possibilities for what you might create:

- A reminder on your phone that pops up daily or weekly
- A card that you can slide into a wallet or phone case
- A background on a phone or other electronic device
- A bookmark that you can place in your Bible or a book that you're reading for school or for leisure
- A card that you can place in the visor of your car

Spend several minutes working on your reminders. Then allow everyone to show their work to one another. Discuss:

- What do you do to remember God and make God part of your daily and weekly routine?
- How do you sometimes forget about God during the course of your day?
- How will this reminder you've created allow you to focus more clearly on your relationship with God?

Looking into the Future (10 minutes)

Supplies: Bibles, a markerboard or large sheet of paper, marker

Though he had spent forty years leading the Israelites out of slavery in Egypt and through the hardships of the wilderness, Moses knew that he would die before the Israelites entered the Promised Land. (See Numbers 20:1-13 for the story.) Even so, Moses was responsible for preparing his fellow Israelites for life in their future home.

Brainstorm things that you are pretty certain will happen but that you probably won't be alive to see—things that you would expect to happen one hundred or more years in the future. This could include things such as interstellar travel, colonizing another planet, or being able to download movies directly to our brains. List these on a markerboard or large sheet of paper.

Once you have a pretty good list, discuss:

- Which of these things would you most like to see happen during your lifetime?
- Are you at all upset by the fact that you probably won't experience certain things during your lifetime?
- Would you be willing to devote much of your life working on something that would not be completed until after your death? Why or why not?

Read Deuteronomy 34:1-12. If possible, take a minute to search "Mount Nebo, Jordan" on phones or other electronic devices to get an idea of what Moses saw when he looked out on the Promised Land. Discuss:

- What did God allow Moses to do before he died?
- What does this Scripture passage tell us about Moses and his importance?
- How do you think Moses felt as he looked out over the Promised Land? What might he have been thinking about or imagining?

Moses had spent his life working for a future that he would not live to see. But before he died, he was blessed with a glimpse of the future he had worked to build. Like Moses, we will not live to see all of God's promises fulfilled. No matter how long we live, there will still be suffering, sin, and injustice. But we can see glimpses of what God has promised. Discuss:

- What things have you witnessed that give you hope for the future?
- What is our congregation doing to address suffering, sin, and injustice in the world? How will our work have an impact on the world well into the future?

The Mountaintop (Optional, 10 minutes)

Supplies: text or video of Martin Luther King Jr.'s "I See the Promised Land" speech (also known as "I've Been to the Mountaintop" speech)

Martin Luther King Jr. gave his final speech at the Mason Temple in Memphis, Tennessee, on April 3, 1968, the night before he was assassinated.

Watch, listen to, or read the last few minutes of this speech. Start at "We've got some difficult days ahead." (If time permits, you might back up and listen to more of the speech.) The full text of the speech is available at the King Center website (www.thekingcenter.org). Many videos of the speech, and particularly of the last few minutes, are available on the Internet. Make sure that the video you choose has been posted legally.

The "mountaintop" King mentions is a reference to Moses and Mount Nebo. Discuss:

- Why do you think King referenced the story of Moses on Mount Nebo?
- What might King have been telling his audience about the future and his part in it?
- Based on what you have read or heard in this speech and what you know about Martin Luther King Jr., what might his vision of the future have looked like?
- In what ways has his vision become a reality? In what ways has his vision not yet been realized?

Spiritual Family Tree (Optional, 10 minutes)

Supplies: large sheet of paper displaying the trunk and branches of a tree, green construction or printer paper, markers

Draw the trunk and branches of a big tree on a large sheet of paper. Cut out leaf shapes from green construction or printer paper. (You can do this beforehand or as a part of the activity.) Have at least three or four leaves for each participant.

Write on your leaves the names of people from previous generations who have had an influence on your faith. This might include parents, adults in your congregation or community, family members, or historical persons who have inspired you by their words or example.

Use tape or glue to attach the leaves to the branches of your tree. As time permits, allow participants to talk about the names they wrote on their leaves and why.

Display your finished tree in your meeting space, both as a way to honor your spiritual ancestors and as a reminder of the influence that you can have on future generations.

Closing Activity: What Now? (10 minutes)

Supplies: a candle that can easily be passed from one person to another

God promises one day to bring an end to sin and death, suffering and injustice. While we might not see this in our future, we can still see how God is working to bring about this reality. We see God's work in the people who address issues such as hunger, poverty, sickness, slavery, and oppression. And we have opportunities to participate in this work and show people how God is alive and active in the world.

As you did in previous sessions, gather in a circle and light a candle. Pass the candle around the circle. When people have the candle, they should name one way they can give people a glimpse of God's promised future through their words, actions, and examples.

After the candle has gone all the way around the circle, have one person hold the candle while the group closes in prayer. (Use the prayer below or one of your own.)

Closing Prayer

God of all things, you have promised us a glorious future. Open our eyes to all the ways that you are working to make this future a reality. We know that we might not see the fulfillment of your promises, but give us the wisdom to know how we can participate in the work you are doing. Bless us as we leave here, that we can apply what we've learned in this study and that the relationships that have developed may continue. Amen.